Daily inspiration
outlook o

CW00501938

365

DAYS

OF

POSITIVE

THINKING

Sarah Ogier

Introduction

Life is not always straightforward; you have ups and downs. Many of us can find stress and challenges in our daily life through work, relationships, or unexpected circumstances. Let's be honest: removing completely those difficulties from your daily life will be challenging. Yet, there are ways to become less impacted emotionally by those hurdles. This book essentially aims to bring a bit of positivity to your daily life through inspiring quotes, positive reminders, and uplifting observations. I highly encourage you to use this book as a daily reminder – in the mornings or evenings – to see life in a brand-new light. Use this book without moderation and simply, be happy, my friend.

Day 1

*« Life is like a bicycle. To keep your **balance**, you must keep moving."*

- Albert Einstein

****

Day 2

Surround yourself with positive and supportive people.

Day 3

Set Meaningful Goals

Set clear and meaningful goals for yourself in your job. Having specific objectives can give you a sense of purpose and motivation to work towards achieving them.

****

Day 4

Communication

Maintain open and honest communication with the people in your life. Be a good listener, express your thoughts and feelings clearly, and be receptive to feedback.

Day 5

Pay for someone's meal or coffee today.

****

Day 6

"Each day provides its own gifts."

- Marcus Aurelius

****

Day 7

Practice gratitude daily by listing things you're thankful for.

Day 8

Find Purpose in Your Work

Connect with the bigger purpose or mission of your job. Understand how your role contributes to the overall goals of your organization and find meaning in the impact you can make.

****

Day 9

Respect

Treat others with respect, regardless of differences or disagreements. Show appreciation for their perspectives, boundaries, and individuality. You will not only learn more about them, but you will also learn more about yourself.

Day 10

Write a heartfelt thank-you note or card for someone today.

****

Day 11

*"Whoever is happy will make others **happy** too."*

- Anne Frank

****

Day 12

Set clear goals for the week or month to come and create an action plan to achieve them.

Day 13

Celebrate Small Wins

Acknowledge and celebrate your accomplishments, no matter how small they may seem. Recognizing your achievements will boost your motivation and confidence.

****

Day 14

Empathy and Understanding

Seek to understand others' perspectives and experiences. Practice empathy by putting yourself in their shoes and showing compassion for their emotions and challenges.

Day 15

Offer to help an elderly or disabled person with their groceries or other tasks today.

****

Day 16

*"Setting goals is the **first step** in turning the invisible into the visible."*

- Tony Robbins

****

Day 17

Break big goals into smaller, manageable tasks. You can do this!

Day 18

Focus on Learning and Growth

View your job as an opportunity for continuous learning and growth. Seek out new challenges, develop new skills, and take advantage of professional development opportunities.

****

Day 19

Active Listening

Practice active listening by giving your full attention when others are speaking. Avoid interrupting them, show interest, and ask questions to show that you genuinely care about what they have to say. They will appreciate and respect you even more in return.

Day 20

Compliment a stranger genuinely and
sincerely today.

****

Day 21

*« Keep your face to the **sunshine** and you cannot
see a shadow. »*

- Helen Keller

****

Day 22

Celebrate your small victories along the
way.

Day 23

Maintain Work-Life Balance

Strive to maintain a healthy work-life balance. Prioritize self-care, set boundaries, and make time for activities outside of work that bring you joy and relaxation.

****

Day 24

Conflict Resolution

Approach conflicts or disagreements with a willingness to find a resolution. Focus on problem-solving rather than winning an argument and be open to compromise and finding common ground. Not always easy to do but always worth the effort.

Day 25

Leave kind and uplifting messages on post-it notes in public places today.

****

Day 26

*"Say something **positive**, and you'll see something **positive**."*

– Jim Thompson

****

Day 27

Find inspiration in books, podcasts, or motivational speeches.

Day 28

Cultivate Positive Relationships

Foster positive relationships with your colleagues and superiors. Surround yourself with supportive and uplifting individuals who can contribute to a positive work environment.

****

Day 29

Forgiveness

Practice forgiveness and let go of grudges. Holding onto resentment can damage relationships, so choose to forgive and move forward.

Day 30

Offer to babysit for a friend or family member this week.

****

Day 31

Donate gently used clothes or items to a local charity or shelter.

****

Day 32

*"You do not find the **happy life**. You make it."*

- Thomas S. Monson

Day 33

Take care of your physical health through regular exercise and a balanced diet.

****

Day 34

Practice Gratitude

Express gratitude for the opportunities and positive aspects of your job. Focus on what you appreciate about your work and the people you work with. There's always a little bit of positive in everything.

Day 35

Practice mindfulness or meditation to calm your mind and **stay present**. If you are a beginner, remember to use free apps or online videos to guide you through it.

****

Day 36

*"Try to be a **rainbow** in someone's cloud."*

- May Angelou

****

Day 37

Send flowers or a small gift to someone who could use a pick-me-up today. This can also be you.

Day 38

*« A winner is a **dreamer** who never gave up »*

- Nelson Mandela

****

Day 39

Embrace failure as a learning opportunity
and a stepping stone to success.

Day 40

Seek Meaningful Connections

Build connections with colleagues who share similar interests or values. Engage in collaborative projects, seek mentorship opportunities, and participate in team-building activities.

****

Day 41

*« Do good and **good** will come to you »*

- Adam Lowy

Day 42

Offer to walk a neighbor's dog or pet-sit for them this week. Yes, dog therapy is a real thing!

****

Day 43

*« Know what sparks the light in you. Then use that light to **illuminate** the world. »*

- Oprah Winfrey

****

Day 44

Focus on your strengths and leverage them in pursuit of your goals.

Day 45

Take Breaks and Recharge

Allow yourself regular breaks throughout the day to recharge and rejuvenate. Stepping away from your work can help maintain focus and prevent burnout.

****

Day 46

"We grow through what we go through."

– Tyrese Gibson

Day 47

*"When you focus on the **good**, the good gets better."*

– Abraham Hicks

****

Day 48

Stay Organized and Prioritize Tasks

Stay organized by creating to-do lists and prioritizing your tasks. Breaking down your workload into manageable steps can help prevent overwhelm and maintain a sense of control.

Day 49

Practice self-care and prioritize your well-being. What can you do for yourself today?

****

Day 50

« *Choose to be **optimistic**, it feels better.* »

- Dalai Lama

Day 51

Embrace Challenges as Opportunities

View challenges and setbacks as
opportunities for growth and learning.
Embrace them as chances to develop
resilience and problem-solving skills.

****

Day 52

Whenever you're feeling sad, just remember
that some of the best days of your life
have not even happened yet.

Day 53

Visualize your success and imagine how achieving your goals will make you feel.

****

Day 54

Practice Positive Self-Talk

Be mindful of your self-talk and cultivate positive and encouraging inner dialogue. Replace negative thoughts with affirmations and focus on your strengths and achievements.

Day 55

*« You only live once, but if you do it **right**, once is enough »*

- Mae West

****

Day 56

Volunteer your time at a local community organization or charity.

****

Day 57

Take breaks and recharge when needed to avoid burnout.

Day 58

*"I must learn to be content with **being happier** than I deserve."*

- Jane Austen

****

Day 59

Seek Feedback and Constructive Criticism

Be open to receiving feedback from your colleagues and superiors. Use it as an opportunity for growth and improvement, and don't take it personally. I know, easier said than done – but not impossible.

Day 60

*"Lay plans for something **big** by starting with it when **small**."*

- Lao Tzu

****

Day 61

Practice deep breathing exercises to reduce stress and increase focus.

Day 62

Take Ownership of Your Work

Take ownership and pride in your work.
Approach tasks with a sense of
responsibility and commitment and strive
for excellence in what you do.

****

Day 63

Embrace challenges as opportunities for
personal growth.

Day 64

*"We all have **two** lives. The second one starts when we realize we only have **one**."*

- Confucius

****

Day 65

Send a care package to a deployed military service member or someone in need this week.

Day 66

*"Many people lose the **small joys** in the hope for the **big happiness.**"*

- Pearl S. Buck

****

Day 67

Embrace Continuous Improvement

Seek ways to improve your work processes and skills. Stay updated on industry trends, seek feedback, and be open to trying new approaches.

Day 68

Develop a **positive morning routine** to set the tone for the day. Yoga, meditation, self-care, listening to your favorite music; you decide.

****

Day 69

"I just think happiness is what makes you pretty. Period. Happy people are beautiful."

- Drew Barrymore

Day 70

Find Inspiration Outside of Work

Look for inspiration and motivation outside of your job. Engage in hobbies, pursue personal interests, and expose yourself to new experiences that can fuel your creativity and enthusiasm.

****

Day 71

Limit exposure to negative news and media.

Day 72

"Keep your face always toward the **sunshine** *—
and shadows will fall behind you."*

- Walt Whitman

****

Day 73

Keep a journal to reflect on your progress
and express your thoughts.

Day 74

Practice Mindfulness at Work

Be present and fully engaged in your work. Practice mindfulness techniques, such as deep breathing or focusing on the task at hand, to stay focused and reduce stress.

****

Day 75

"Hardships often prepare ordinary people for an extraordinary destiny."

— C.S. Lewis

Day 76

Find a hobby or activity that brings you joy
and helps you relax.

****

Day 77

*"All you need is the plan, the road map, and the
courage to press on to your destination."*

- Earl Nightingal

****

Day 78

Offer to help a coworker with a task or
project they're struggling with.

Day 79

Take Initiative and Seek New Challenges

Look for opportunities to take on new responsibilities or projects that stretch your capabilities. Taking initiative can keep you motivated and help you grow in your career.

****

Day 80

Seek feedback and **constructive** criticism to improve yourself.

Day 81

The only way to do great work is to love what you do."

- Steve Jobs

****

Day 82

Hold the door open for someone or give up your seat on public transportation today.

****

Day 83

Stay organized and manage your time effectively.

Day 84

*"**Positive** thinking will let you do everything better than **negative** thinking will."*

- Zig Ziglar

****

Day 85

Practice forgiveness, both towards yourself and others.

Day 86

*"Believe you can and you're **halfway** there."*

- Theodore Roosevelt

****

Day 87

Write positive reviews for local businesses
you enjoy.

****

Day 88

Embrace a **growth mindset** and believe in
your ability to learn and improve.

Day 89

Avoid Negative Influences

Surround yourself with positivity and distance yourself from negative influences or toxic relationships in the workplace. Choose to spend time with colleagues who uplift and support you.

****

Day 90

"In the middle of difficulty lies opportunity."

- Albert Einstein

Day 91

Surround yourself with inspirational quotes
or images in your workspace.

****

Day 92

Reflect on Your Accomplishments

Regularly reflect on your achievements and
the progress you've made in your job. This
reflection can boost your motivation and
remind you of the value you bring to your
work.

Day 93

Express **appreciation and gratitude** for the people in your life. Recognize their contributions, support, and kindness, and let them know how much they mean to you.

****

Day 94

Take small steps **forward** consistently, even when progress feels slow.

****

Day 95

"The best way to predict the future is to create it."

- Peter Drucker

Day 96

Be supportive and encourage others in their endeavors. Offer help when needed, provide words of encouragement, and celebrate their **successes**.

****

Day 97

Focus on the present moment and avoid dwelling on past mistakes or future worries.

Day 98

Respect **personal boundaries** and establish your own. Communicate your limits and expectations clearly and be mindful of others' boundaries.

****

Day 99

Develop a **morning gratitude practice** to start your day on a positive note.

Day 100

*"Success is not the key to happiness. Happiness is the key to success. If you **love** what you are doing, you will be **successful**."*

- Albert Schweitzer

****

Day 101

Build trust by being reliable and keeping your commitments. Be someone others can count on and maintain confidentiality when appropriate.

Day 102

Help others and engage in **acts of kindness** and generosity.

****

Day 103

Organize a fundraiser or participate in a charity event for a cause you care about.

****

Day 104

"The only limit to our realization of tomorrow will be our doubts of today."

- Franklin D. Roosevelt

Day 105

Take care of your mental health by seeking support when needed.

****

Day 106

Make time for quality interactions and meaningful connections. Prioritize spending time with loved ones, engaging in activities together, and creating shared experience.

Day 107

*"Positive **anything** is better than negative nothing."*

- Elbert Hubbard

****

Day 108

Find a mentor or role model who can guide and inspire you.

Day 109

Maintain a **healthy balance** between giving and receiving in relationships. Avoid being overly dependent or solely focused on your own needs and be attentive to the needs of others.

****

Day 110

"For every minute you are angry you lose sixty seconds of happiness."

– Ralph Waldo Emerson

Day 111

Practice **positive self-talk** and replace negative thoughts with empowering ones.

✳✳✳✳

Day 112

*"The greatest discovery of all time is that a person can **change their future** by merely changing their attitude."*

- Oprah Winfrey

Day 113

Be yourself and encourage others to be authentic as well. Embrace **vulnerability** and **honesty** in your interactions to foster genuine connections.

****

Day 114

Embrace challenges as opportunities for growth and resilience.

Day 115

*"In all of living, have much fun and laughter. Life is to be **enjoyed**, not just endured."*

– Gordon B. Hinchley

****

Day 116

Cultivate a positive attitude and bring positivity into your relationships. Be supportive, uplifting, and focus on the strengths and positive aspects of others.

Day 117

*"You don't stop **laughing** because you grow older. You grow older because you stop laughing."*

— Maurice Chevalier

****

Day 118

Stay curious and continue learning new things.

Day 119

*"The **pessimist** sees difficulty in every opportunity.
The **optimist** sees opportunity in every difficulty."*

- Winston Churchill

****

Day 120

Practice time management techniques to
stay productive and motivated.

Day 121

Embrace and celebrate the differences in others. Recognize and appreciate diverse perspectives, cultures, and backgrounds.

****

Day 122

Surround yourself with uplifting and motivational music.

Day 123

Take responsibility for your mistakes and apologize when necessary. Show genuine remorse and make amends to **rebuild trust** and maintain positive relationships.

****

Day 124

"A positive attitude causes a chain reaction of positive thoughts, events, and outcomes. It is a catalyst, and it sparks extraordinary results."

- Wade Boggs

Day 125

Offer to give someone a ride who doesn't have transportation today.

****

Day 126

Set realistic expectations and **avoid comparing yourself** to others.

****

Day 127

Be thoughtful and considerate in your actions and words. Show **kindness**, offer help when needed, and remember important dates or occasions.

Day 128

"Laughter is the sound of the soul dancing."

– Jarod Kintz

****

Day 129

Break tasks into smaller, more manageable steps. Things will feel much more doable.

****

Day 130

"Your time is limited, don't waste it living someone else's life."

- Steve Jobs

Day 131

Be open to change and willing to adapt in relationships. Recognize that people grow and evolve and be flexible in adjusting to new dynamics.

****

Day 132

Seek inspiration from nature and spend time outdoors.

****

Day 133

"A smile is a curve that sets everything straight."

- Phyllis Diller

Day 134

Use humor to lighten the mood and create a positive atmosphere. Laugh together, share jokes, and find joy in lighthearted moments.

****

Day 135

"The future belongs to those who believe in the beauty of their dreams."

- Eleanor Roosevelt

Day 136

"The best way to cheer yourself up is to try to cheer somebody else up."

- Mark Twain

****

Day 137

Regularly check in with the important people in your life. Ask how they're doing, listen attentively, and offer your support. Showing you care is important.

Day 138

Create a vision board or visual
representation of your goals and dreams.

****

Day 139

*"Choose a job you love, and you will **never** have to
work a day in your life."*

- Confucius

****

Day 140

Bake cookies or treats and share them with
your neighbors or coworkers this week.

Day 141

*"A day without **laughter** is a day wasted."*

- Charlie Chaplin

****

Day 142

*"Happiness is not something you postpone for the future; it is something you design for the **present**."*

- Jim Rohn

Day 143

"The positive thinker sees the invisible, feels the intangible, and achieves the impossible."

- Winston Churchill

****

Day 144

"You're never too old to be young."

- Snow White

****

Day 145

"The only way to have a friend is to be one."

- Ralph Waldo Emerson

Day 146

"When in doubt, just take the next small step."

- Paulo Coelho

****

Day 147

"I have a simple philosophy: Fill what's empty. Empty what's full. Scratch where it itches."

- Alice Roosevelt Longworth

Day 148

Take regular breaks to rest and recharge
your energy.

****

Day 149

*"Don't watch the clock; do what it does. **Keep
going**."*

- Sam Levenson

Day 150

Practice Time Management

Develop effective time management skills to prioritize tasks, reduce stress, and create a healthy work-life balance. Use tools such as to-do lists, calendars, or time-blocking techniques to stay organized.

****

Day 151

*"The most important thing is to **enjoy your life** — to be happy. It's all that matters."*

— Audrey Hepburn

Day 152

"The mind is everything. What you think, you become."

– Buddha

****

Day 153

"Nothing can bring you happiness but yourself."

– Ralph Waldo Emerson

Day 154

*"Your **attitude**, not your aptitude, will determine your altitude."*

- Zig Ziglar

****

Day 155

Offer to tutor or mentor a student who could use some extra help.

****

Day 156

Celebrate your progress and acknowledge your achievements, no matter how small.

Day 157

*"Never regret anything that made you **smile**."*

– Mark Twain

✳✳✳✳

Day 158

Today, focus on stressing less and feeling blessed.

✳✳✳✳

Day 159

Reflect on your values and align your actions with them.

Day 160

"You are never too old to set another goal or to dream a new dream."

- C.S. Lewis

****

Day 161

Practice Good Hygiene

Maintain good personal hygiene habits, such as regular handwashing, dental care, and skincare. These simple practices contribute to overall health and well-being.

Day 162

"Happiness is the best makeup."

– Drew Barrymore

****

Day 163

Practice positive affirmations to boost your self-belief.

Day 164

*"Positive thinking is more than just a tagline. It changes the way we behave. And I firmly believe that when I am positive, it not only makes me better, but it also makes those around me **better**."*

- Harvey Mackay

****

Day 165

*"Happiness is a **state of mind**. It's just according to the way you look at things."*

– Walt Disney

Day 166

"If you want to be happy, be."

– Leo Tolstoy

****

Day 167

"Independence is happiness."

– Susan B. Anthony

****

Day 168

Keep a gratitude journal to focus on the
positives in your life.

Day 169

"Success is not final, failure is not fatal: It is the courage to continue that counts."

- Winston Churchill

****

Day 170

Volunteer or Give Back

Engage in acts of kindness and service to others. Volunteering or giving back to your community can provide a sense of purpose and fulfillment.

Day 171

Avoid negative self-talk and cultivate a mindset of self-compassion.

✻✻✻✻

Day 172

Send a handwritten letter or card to a friend or family member who lives far away.

✻✻✻✻

Day 173

"Simplicity makes me happy."

– Alicia Keys

Day 174

Surround yourself with supportive and positive people.

****

Day 175

"Positive thoughts lead to positive actions, and positive actions lead to positive outcomes."

- Zig Ziglar

****

Day 176

Happiness is simply seeing life for what it is, in all the **big** and **little** moments.

Day 177

*"Happiness is when what you think, what you say, and what you do are in **harmony**."*

– Mahatma Gandhi

****

Day 178

Embrace Nature

Spend time in nature and soak in its beauty. Whether it's going for a hike, gardening, or simply enjoying a walk in the park, connecting with nature can have positive effects on your well-being.

Day 179

"Believe in yourself and all that you are. Know that there is something inside you that is greater than any obstacle."

- Christian D. Larson

****

Day 180

Clean up litter in your neighborhood or a local park.

****

Day 181

Stay flexible and open-minded in the face of challenges and setbacks.

Day 182

The happiness you're looking for is all around you, simply don't forget to notice it.

****

Day 183

"You miss 100% of the shots you don't take."

- Wayne Gretzky

Day 184

*"Happiness is the secret to all beauty. There is no beauty without **happiness.**"*

— Christian Dior

****

Day 185

Remember that motivation comes and goes, but **discipline** and **commitment** will keep you going.

Day 186

"Happiness isn't a goal... it's a by-product of a life well lived."

— Eleanor Roosevelt

****

Day 187

Laugh and Have Fun

Incorporate laughter and playfulness into your life. Surround yourself with humor, engage in activities that make you laugh, and don't take yourself too seriously.

Day 188

*"Optimism is the faith that leads to achievement. Nothing can be done without **hope** and **confidence**."*

- Helen Keller

****

Day 189

Offer to do someone's chores or errands for them when they're feeling overwhelmed.

Day 190

"There is no path to happiness. Happiness is the path."

– Buddha

* * * *

Day 191

Being happy is actually very **simple**: the secret is to find peace where you are even if you're not yet where you want to be.

Day 192

Prioritize Self-Care

Make self-care a priority in your daily routine. Engage in activities that bring you joy and help you relax, such as taking a bath, reading a book, or practicing mindfulness.

****

Day 193

*"The only place where your **dream** becomes impossible is in your own thinking."*

- Robert H. Schuller

Day 194

*"The only thing that will make you happy is being happy with **who you are**."*

– Goldie Hawn

****

Day 195

The **happiest** people make the best of what they have instead of craving what they don't. Focus on the positive around you and the positivity will come around.

Day 196

Practice Mindfulness

Incorporate mindfulness into your daily life. Take a few moments each day to focus on your breath and be fully present in the moment.

****

Day 197

True happiness is found by living in the present moment. Take 2 minutes now to truly feel present.

Day 198

*« If **opportunity** doesn't knock, build a door."*

- Milton Berle

****

Day 199

Leave a generous tip for your server or
barista today.

Day 200

Stay Active

Engage in regular physical exercise, as it can boost your mood, reduce stress, and improve your overall mental well-being.

****

Day 201

"Real happiness is cheap enough, yet how dearly we pay for it is counterfeit."

– Hosea Ballou

Day 202

*"The only limit to our **realization** of tomorrow will be our **doubts** of today."*

- Franklin D. Roosevelt

****

Day 203

Get Enough Sleep

Prioritize getting enough quality sleep each night. Establish a bedtime routine, create a comfortable sleep environment, and avoid screens before bed to promote better sleep.

Day 204

"You can, you should, and if you're brave enough to start, you will."

- Stephen King

****

Day 205

Share your knowledge or skills by offering free lessons or workshops.

Day 206

Establish Healthy Boundaries

Set boundaries in your personal and professional life to avoid burnout and maintain a healthy work-life balance. Learn to say no when necessary and prioritize your well-being.

****

Day 207

"There is only one happiness in life, to love and be loved."

– George Sand

Day 208

"Keep your face always toward the sunshine and the shadow will fall behind you."

– Walt Whitman

****

Day 209

Practice Positivity on Social Media

Be mindful of your social media use and curate your online experience to promote positivity. Follow accounts that inspire and uplift you, and limit exposure to negative or triggering content.

Day 210

"Positive thoughts breed positive results."

- Zig Ziglar

****

Day 211

"True happiness is found inside the heart."

— Anurag Prakash Ray

Day 212

Reach out to friends, family, or a therapist when you need support. Talking about your feelings and concerns can help alleviate stress and provide perspective.

✳✳✳✳

Day 213

*"True happiness... is not attained through self-gratification, but through fidelity to a **worthy purpose**."*

– Helen Keller

Day 214

Being grateful for what you have leads you
toward true happiness. What are you
grateful for today?

****

Day 215

Practice Relaxation Techniques

Explore relaxation techniques such as deep
breathing exercises, meditation, or yoga to
reduce stress and promote relaxation.

Day 216

"The greatest weapon against stress is our ability to choose one thought over another."

- William James

****

Day 217

"Happiness is the spiritual experience of living every minute with love, grace, and gratitude."

– Denis Waitley

Day 218

*"True happiness arises, in the first place, from the enjoyment of **one's self,** and in the next, from the friendship and conversation of **a few select companions."***

– Joseph Addison

****

Day 219

"Life is short. Smile while you still have teeth."

– Mallory Hopkins

Day 220

Limit Exposure to News

Limit your exposure to news and social media, especially if it triggers anxiety or stress. Set boundaries for yourself and focus on positive and uplifting content.

****

Day 221

"The most wasted of all days is one without laughter."

– E.E. Cummings

Day 222

"Trouble knocked at the door, but hearing laughter, hurried away."

– Benjamin Franklin

* * * *

Day 223

"Laughter is timeless, imagination has no age, and dreams are forever."

– Walt Disney

Day 224

*"The difference between ordinary and extraordinary
is that little extra."*

- Jimmy Johnson

****

Day 225

Send a surprise gift or care package to a
friend who's going through a difficult time.

****

Day 226

"Laughter is an instant **vacation**."

— Milton Berle

Day 227

"Be somebody who makes everyone feel like a somebody."

– Courtney Shields

****

Day 228

Nourish Your Body

Eat a balanced diet that includes nutrient-rich foods to support your overall well-being. Stay hydrated and limit the consumption of substances that can negatively impact your mental health, such as alcohol or excessive caffeine.

Day 229

"The biggest adventure you can take is to live the life of your dreams."

- Oprah Winfrey

****

Day 230

Offer to pick up groceries or prescriptions for someone who is unable to do so themselves.

Day 231

*"Some days you just have to create your **own** sunshine."*

– Sam Sundquist

****

Day 232

Challenge Negative Thoughts

Be aware of negative thoughts and challenge them with positive and realistic ones. Practice reframing negative thinking patterns to promote a more positive mindset.

Day 233

*"It's not how much we have but **how much we enjoy** that makes happiness."*

– Charles Spurgeon

****

Day 234

"Don't cry because it's over, smile because it happened."

– Dr. Seuss

Day 235

"If you see someone without a smile, give them one of yours."

– Dolly Parton

✳✳✳✳

Day 236

"Smile at strangers and you just might change a life."

– Masashi Kishimoto

Day 237

*"Success is not in what you have, but **who you are**."*

- Bo Bennett

****

Day 238

"Peace begins with a smile."

– Mother Teresa

Day 239

"A simple smile. That's the start of opening your heart and being **compassionate** *to others."*

— Dalai Lama

****

Day 240

Engage in Hobbies

Dedicate time to activities you enjoy and that bring you a sense of fulfillment. Engaging in hobbies can provide a sense of purpose and help you unwind.

Day 241

"She was trouble, chaos really, but her smile, her smile dared me to fall in love with her."

– Atticus

＊＊＊＊

Day 242

*"To fall in love with **yourself** is the first secret to happiness."*

– Robert Morley

Day 243

"So many people love you. Don't focus on the people that don't."

– Soyen

****

Day 244

*"The only person you should try to be better than is the person you were **yesterday**."*

- Matty Mullins

Day 245

Share inspirational or uplifting quotes on social media to brighten someone's day.

****

Day 246

"Forgive yourself for not having the foresight to know what seems so obvious in hindsight."

– Judy Belmont

Day 247

"Wouldn't it be powerful if you fell in love with yourself so deeply that you would do just about anything if you knew it would make you happy? This is precisely how much life loves you and wants you to nurture yourself. The deeper you love yourself, the more the universe will affirm your worth. Then you can enjoy a lifelong love affair that brings you the richest fulfillment from inside out."

– Alan Cohen

Day 248

Cultivate a Supportive Network

Surround yourself with positive and supportive people who uplift you and provide a sense of belonging. Foster meaningful connections and engage in social activities that bring you joy.

****

Day 249

"The only thing standing between you and your goal is the story you keep telling yourself as to why you can't achieve it."

- Jordan Belfort

Day 250

Help a stranger struggling with heavy bags
or luggage this week.

****

Day 251

*"The best revenge is to have enough **self-worth** not
to seek it."*

– Courtney Jarvis

****

Day 252

*"Happiness is not something ready-made. It comes
from your **own actions**."*

– Dalai Lama

Day 253

"The key to being happy is knowing you have the power to choose what to accept and what to let go."

— Dodinsky

****

Day 254

"If you ever have to decide between winning a fight or being happy, choose happiness. Being happy automatically makes you a winner."

— Karen Salmansohn

Day 255

*"Don't be afraid to give up the **good** to go for the great."*

- John D. Rockefeller

****

Day 256

Practice Gratitude

Cultivate a practice of gratitude by regularly acknowledging and appreciating the positive aspects of your life. This can be done through journaling, creating a gratitude list, or expressing gratitude to others.

Day 257

"I have witnessed the softening of the hardest of hearts by a simple smile."

– Goldie Hawn

* * * *

Day 258

*"Never feel guilty for doing what's **best for you**."*

– Dushant Isankar

Day 259

"Happiness is the highest form of health."

– Dalai Lama

****

Day 260

Leave positive reviews or comments on social media for small businesses you support this week.

****

Day 261

*"Turn your wounds into **wisdom**"*

– Oprah

Day 262

Set Realistic Goals

Set realistic and achievable goals for yourself. Break them down into smaller, manageable steps to maintain motivation and a sense of accomplishment.

****

Day 263

*"Try to be a **rainbow** in someone else's cloud."*

– Maya Angelou

Day 264

"Be happy for this moment. This moment is your life."

– Omar Khayyam

****

Day 265

"We all have two lives. The second one starts when we realize we only have one."

– Tom Hiddleston

Day 266

"If it comes, let it come. If it stays, let it stay. If it goes, let it go."

– Nicholas Sparks

****

Day 267

*"Happiness is an **attitude**. We either make ourselves miserable, or happy and strong. The amount of work is the same."*

- Francesca Reigler

Day 268

"Whoever is happy will make others happy."

– Anne Frank

****

Day 269

"I have what I have. And I am happy. I have lost what I've lost. And I am still happy."

– Rupi Kaur

Day 270

Disconnect and Unplug

Take regular breaks from technology and digital devices. Disconnecting can help reduce stress, improve focus, and promote mindfulness.

****

Day 271

*"You don't need too many people to be happy, just a few **real ones** who appreciate you for **who you** are."*

– Wiz Khalifa

Day 272

"Being happy isn't having everything in your life be perfect. Maybe it's about stringing together all the little things."

— Ann Brashares

****

Day 273

"Joy is what happens to us when we allow ourselves to recognize how good things really are."

— Marianne Williamson

Day 274

"Your life does not get better by chance; it gets better by change."

- Jim Rohn

* * * *

Day 275

Offer to listen and provide emotional support to someone who needs to talk.

Day 276

"A sure way to lose happiness, I found, is to want it at the expense of everything else."

– Bette Davis

****

Day 277

*"If you want to live a happy life, tie it to a **goal**, not to people or things."*

– Albert Einstein

Day 278

"Happiness is a place between too much and too little."

– Finnish Proverb

****

Day 279

Engage in Positive Self-Talk

Be mindful of your self-talk and practice speaking to yourself with kindness and compassion. Replace self-criticism with self-encouragement and affirmations.

Day 280

*« A positive attitude causes a chain reaction of positive thoughts, events, and outcomes. It is a catalyst, and it sparks **extraordinary results**."*

\- Wade Boggs

****

Day 281

"The pleasure which we most rarely experience gives us greatest delight."

– Epictetus

Day 282

"Count your age by friends, not years. Count your life by smiles, not tears."

– John Lennon

****

Day 283

"No matter how hard the past, you can always begin again."

– Buddha

Day 284

Practice Assertiveness

Learn to communicate your needs, opinions, and boundaries assertively. This can help reduce stress, improve relationships, and promote self-respect.

****

Day 285

Give someone a genuine and heartfelt compliment about their character or actions.

Day 286

"Life is a great big canvas; throw all the paint you can on it."

- Danny Kaye

****

Day 287

*"If you obey all the rules, you'll miss all the **fun**."*

- Katharine Hepburn

Day 288

"Life has no limitations, except the ones you make."

- Les Brown

****

Day 289

"A positive attitude may not solve all your problems, but it will annoy enough people to make it worth the effort."

- Herm Albright

Day 290

Seek Help When Needed

If you're struggling with your mental health,
don't hesitate to seek professional help.
Reach out to a therapist or counselor who
can provide guidance and support.

****

Day 291

*"Enjoy the **little things** in life, for one day you
may look back and realize they were the **big
things.**"*

- Robert Breault

Day 292

*"One way to get the most out of life is to look upon it as an **adventure**."*

- William Feather

****

Day 293

*"The **purpose of life**, after all, is to live it, to taste experience to the utmost, to reach out eagerly and without fear for newer and richer experiences."*

- Eleanor Roosevelt

Day 294

"Happiness is not something ready-made. It comes from your own actions."

- Dalai Lama

****

Day 295

"The saddest summary of a life contains three descriptions: could have, might have, and should have."

- Louis E. Boone

Day 296

*"Living in the moment means **letting go of the past** and not waiting for the future. It means living your life **consciously**, aware that each moment you breathe is a **gift**."*

- Oprah Winfrey

****

Day 297

"Every moment in our lives is a miracle we should enjoy instead of ignoring."

- Yoko Ono

Day 298

Engage in Activities that Bring You Joy

Identify activities that bring you joy and make time for them regularly. Engaging in enjoyable activities can boost your mood and overall well-being.

****

Day 299

Surprise a coworker with their favorite snack or treat this week.

Day 300

*"A **positive attitude** gives you power over your circumstances instead of your circumstances having power over you."*

- Joyce Meyer

****

Day 301

*"The journey is never-ending. There's always gonna be growth, improvement, adversity; you just gotta take it all in and do what's right, continue to grow, continue to **live in the moment**."*

- Antonio Brown

Day 302

*"I don't have to chase extraordinary moments to find **happiness**—it's right in front of me if I'm paying attention and practicing gratitude."*

- Brené Brown

* * * *

Day 303

"Life is about not knowing, having to change, taking the moment and making the best of it, without knowing what's going to happen next."

- Gilda Radner

Day 304

Embrace Imperfection
Accept that nobody is perfect, including yourself. Embrace imperfections, learn from mistakes, and practice self-compassion.

****

Day 305

Offer to teach someone a new skill or hobby you're passionate about this month.

Day 306

"That man is rich whose pleasures are the cheapest."

- Henry David Thoreau

****

Day 307

"Let your boat of life be light, packed with only what you need—a homely home and simple pleasures, one or two friends, worth the name, someone to love and someone to love you, a cat, a dog, and a pipe or two, enough to eat and enough to wear, and a little more than enough to drink; for thirst is a dangerous thing."

- Jerome K. Jerome

Day 308

"As I've grown older, the simple pleasure of sitting on the couch with someone you love and watching a documentary is about as good as it gets for me."

- Paul Wesley

****

Day 309

"Good friends, good books, and a sleepy conscience: this is the ideal life."

- Mark Twain

Day 310

*"**Simple pleasures** are the last healthy refuge in a complex world."*

- Oscar Wilde

****

Day 311

Prioritize Self-Care

Make self-care a priority by incorporating activities that nourish your mind, body, and soul into your routine. This may include activities like exercise, meditation, reading, or spending time in nature.

Day 312

Share a book you love by giving it as a gift or leaving it in a public place for someone to find.

****

Day 313

"In this age of getting what you want and getting it now, the simple pleasure of browsing is often forgotten."

- Tom Hodgkinson

Day 314

*"Today, just **take time** to smell the roses, enjoy those little things about your life, your family, spouse, friends, job. Forget about the thorns—the pains and problems they cause you—and enjoy life."*

- Bernard Kelvin Clive

* * * *

Day 315

"You have to enjoy life. Always be surrounded by people that you like, people who have a nice conversation. There are so many positive things to think about."

- Sophia Loren

Day 316

*"I think people should **have fun**. And don't get so down on yourself. Enjoy life and be the best person you can be."*

- Keke Palmer

****

Day 317

*"Perfect happiness is a beautiful sunset, the giggle of a grandchild, the first snowfall. It's the **little things** that make happy moments, not the grand events. Joy comes in sips, not gulps."*

- Sharon Draper

Day 318

"Life is a journey, and if you fall in love with the journey, you will be in love forever."

- Peter Hagerty

****

Day 319

Maintain a Balanced Diet

Eat a balanced diet that includes a variety of whole foods such as fruits, vegetables, whole grains, lean proteins, and healthy fats. Limit processed foods, sugary snacks, and drinks.

Day 320

Donate blood or register as an organ donor to help save lives this week.

****

Day 321

Stay Active

Engage in regular physical activity that you enjoy. Aim for at least 150 minutes of moderate-intensity exercise or 75 minutes of vigorous exercise per week. Find activities that fit your interests and lifestyle.

Day 322

*"Life is an **opportunity**, seize the day, live each day to the fullest. Life is not a project, but a journey to be enjoyed."*

- Catherine Pulsifer

* * * *

Day 323

*"I made up my mind not to care so much about the destination, and simply enjoy the **journey**."*

- David Archuleta

Day 324

"Aim for the sky, but move slowly, enjoying every step along the way. It is all those little steps that make the journey complete."

- Chanda Kochhar

****

Day 325

"I don't have to be perfect. All I have to do is show up and enjoy the messy, imperfect, and beautiful journey of my life."

- Kerry Washington

Day 326

Get Enough Sleep

Prioritize getting quality sleep. Aim for 7-9 hours of sleep each night to support overall health and well-being. Establish a bedtime routine and create a sleep-friendly environment.

****

Day 327

"A good traveler has no fixed plans and is not intent on arriving."

– Laozi

Day 328

"There are three things that grow more precious with age; old wood to burn, old books to read, and old friends to enjoy."

- Henry Ford

****

Day 329

*"Getting to know new people and gaining new friends is one of life's **greatest pleasures**. So conquer your fears and get out there."*

- Tony Clark

Day 330

Offer to help a parent with young children
by watching their kids for a few hours.

****

Day 331

Practice Stress Management

Find effective ways to manage stress, such
as practicing relaxation techniques,
engaging in hobbies, journaling, or seeking
support from friends, family, or a therapist.

Day 332

"Life is partly what we make it, and partly what it is made by the friends we choose."

- Tennessee Williams

****

Day 333

"I cannot even imagine where I would be today were it not for that handful of friends who have given me a heart full of joy. Let's face it, friends make life a lot more fun."

- Charles R. Swindoll

Day 334

"The love that comes from friendship is the underlying facet of a happy life."

- Chelsea Handler

****

Day 335

"Find a group of people who challenge and inspire you; spend a lot of time with them, and it will change your life."

- Amy Poehler

Day 336

Foster Positive Relationships

Surround yourself with positive and supportive people who uplift and inspire you. Nurture meaningful connections and invest time and effort into maintaining strong relationships.

****

Day 337

*"Your body cannot heal without **play**. Your mind cannot heal without **laughter**. Your soul cannot heal without **joy**."*

- Catherine Rippenger Fenwick

Day 338

"If you don't want to be sad and sorry all your life, learn how to laugh at yourself."

- Marty Rubin

* * * *

Day 339

"I've always thought that a big laugh is a really loud noise from the soul saying, "Ain't that the truth."

- Quincy Jones

Day 340

Send a handwritten note of appreciation to a teacher or mentor who made a positive impact on your life.

****

Day 341

Set Realistic Goals

Set achievable goals that align with your values and aspirations. Break them down into smaller, manageable steps, and celebrate your progress along the way.

Day 342

"Laughter is therapy for physical pain, emotional pain, and the everyday pain of life."

- Terri Guillemets

****

Day 343

"A good time to laugh is any time you can."

- Linda Ellerbee

Day 344

"Happiness, laughter, and joy abound, when friends, family, and lovers are around."

- Amy Davis

****

Day 345

Offer to help a friend or family member with home repairs or renovations.

Day 346

"When we laugh at the joy in everyday life we realize that the world is not such a serious place after all."

- Dee Waldeck

****

Day 347

Practice Mindfulness

Cultivate mindfulness by being fully present in the moment. Engage in activities that promote mindfulness, such as meditation, deep breathing exercises, or yoga.

Day 348

*"To get the full value of joy, you must have **someone** to divide it with."*

- Mark Twain

****

Day 349

*"Once we recognize what it is we are feeling, once we recognize we can feel deeply, love deeply, can feel joy, then we will demand that all parts of our lives produce **that kind of joy.**"*

- Audre Lorde

Day 350

"The best thing to hold onto in life is each other."

- Audrey Hepburn

****

Day 351

Limit Screen Time

Be mindful of your screen time and set boundaries around your use of electronic devices. Allocate time for unplugging and engaging in activities that don't involve screens.

Day 352

Give someone a sincere and warm hug to show you care today.

****

Day 353

"One word frees us of all the weight and pain of life. That word is love."

– Sophocles

Day 354

"When you cultivate quality relationships, not only do you feel better and help your friends feel better, but you contribute to an increase of joy, love, and peace in the world."

- Tara Bianca

****

Day 355

Hydrate

Drink an adequate amount of water each day to stay hydrated. Carry a water bottle with you and make it a habit to drink water throughout the day.

Day 356

*"You cannot protect yourself from **sadness** without protecting yourself from **happiness.**"*

- Jonathan Safran Foer

✳✳✳✳

Day 357

Share your umbrella with someone on a rainy or snowy day.

Day 358

Engage in Lifelong Learning

Foster a curious mindset and embrace
opportunities for continuous learning and
personal growth. Engage in activities that
expand your knowledge and skills.

****

Day 359

"No medicine cures what happiness cannot."

- Gabriel García Márquez

Day 360

If possible, offer to mow your neighbor's lawn or shovel snow from their driveway this week.

****

Day 361

"Nothing really matters except what you do now in this instant of time."

- Eileen Caddy

Day 362

"True happiness is an inner power — natural, healing, abundant and always available."

- Robert Holden

****

Day 363

"Don't wait around for other people to be happy for you. Any happiness you get you've got to make yourself."

- Alice Walker

Day 364

Engage in Hobbies and Recreation

Dedicate time to activities that bring you
joy and relaxation. Engaging in hobbies,
creative pursuits, or recreational activities
can help reduce stress and promote a sense
of fulfillment.

****

Day 365

Be proud of yourself for seeking happiness
in your life. A year has now passed, and I
truly hope this book helped you open your
eyes to all the existent beauty present
around you. Be kind to yourself and share
the positivity now to others.

Printed in Great Britain
by Amazon